To Kimberly

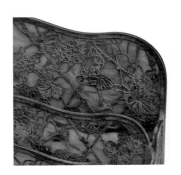

AMERICAN
FROM THE COLLECTION OF

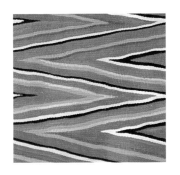

ARTS & CRAFTS
ALEXANDRA & SIDNEY SHELDON

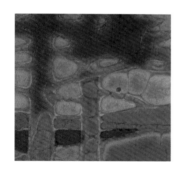

Palm Springs Desert Museum   Palm Springs, California

AMERICAN ARTS AND CRAFTS FROM
THE COLLECTION OF ALEXANDRA AND
SIDNEY SHELDON

*This project is funded in part by the Palm
Springs Desert Museum's Western Art Council*

Palm Springs Desert Museum
February 17–June 6, 1993

Published by the
Palm Springs Desert Museum
101 Museum Drive
Palm Springs, California 92262

Distributed by
University of Washington Press
P.O. Box 50096
Seattle, Washington 98145-5096

Library of Congress Cataloging-in-Publication Data

Hough, Katherine Plake.
     American arts and crafts from the collection of Alexandra and
   Sidney Sheldon / Katherine Plake Hough.
          p.   cm.
       An exhibition catalog.
       Includes bibliographical references.
        1. Arts and crafts movement — United States — Exhibitions.
     2. Decorative arts — United States — History — 20th century —
     Exhibitions. 3. Sheldon, Alexandra — Art collections — Exhibitions.
     4. Sheldon, Sidney — Art collections — Exhibitions. 5. Decorative
     arts — Private collections — California — Palm Springs — Exhibitions.
     6. Palm Springs Desert Museum — Exhibitions. I. Title.
     NK1141.H68 1993
     745'.0973'07479497 — dc20   92-40714
                                                                 CIP

ISBN 295-97280-7

cover:
Grueby Pottery, Boston, Massachusetts,
1907-1913
VASE (detail)
ceramic, matte green glaze with yellow
raised flower buds
h: 6¾; dia: 4½ inches
catalog no. 98

Table of Contents

Foreword

We at the Palm Springs Desert Museum are graced by the presence of Alexandra and Sidney Sheldon as neighbors and supporters. Their long-standing residency in Palm Springs is an example of the artistic and cultural sophistication to be found here, and we are most fortunate that the Sheldons, in turn, have found us. To know them is to realize the depth of their passion for the arts.

Both Alexandra and Sidney are collectors, each with a chosen emphasis. It is primarily Alexandra's passion, however, that runs to the American Arts and Crafts Movement. The Sheldon collection of furniture, objects and paintings by western artists, craftsmen and Native Americans complements a component of the Museum's expressed mission to emphasize and interpret the arts of the western United States.

Alexandra and Sidney have collected with discrimination and intelligence. This exhibition is especially valuable in that it affords a thorough overview of the American Arts and Crafts Movement. Superb examples are placed in tableaux to re-create the ambiance of the period.

Craftsman exhibitions appear infrequently, and they are usually achieved by borrowing works from many sources. It's rare to find a collection that has been as meticulously assembled as the one assembled by the Sheldons, rarer still for works of such fine quality to be made available for public exhibition and with as much enthusiasm. The story of the American Arts and Crafts Movement has been laid out from a single source, and the Sheldons deserve our warmest congratulations and appreciation for making it possible.

I also want to congratulate and thank Katherine Plake Hough, our Curator of Art, for her curatorial work in the face of extremely tight deadlines. With assistance from a dedicated Art Department staff, she successfully and expertly juggled the intricate details of selection, research, catalog essay and exhibition design responsibilities.

Along with the entire Board of Trustees and staff of the Palm Springs Desert Museum, I welcome you to this exceptional exhibition, *American Arts and Crafts from the Collection of Alexandra and Sidney Sheldon*.

Fritz A. Frauchiger
Director

Collectors Preface

Alexandra and Sidney Sheldon
photography by Alan Berlinger,
Los Angeles

As a young child I emulated my older sister, Mary, and by the tender age of ten my desire was to be able to communicate with her on subjects she was studying in college. I read her textbooks about philosophy, design, architecture, etc. This was my introduction to the wonderful world of Frank Lloyd Wright, his feeling about the importance of natural light in architecture, his Prairie school design homes in Oak Park, Illinois, and his beautiful Prairie school oak furniture. I became nearly obsessed with Frank Lloyd Wright and found every book that I could about him, devouring every word.

As a very young child I also had a passion for the Native American. At the age of five, I would storm out of a movie theater if the film portrayed a negative image of Indians. When I was twelve, I was slapped by a teacher because I stood up during a lecture that he was giving that was derogatory about Indians, and I gave an impassioned speech defending Native Americans pointing out their spirituality, wisdom of the land and nature and the beauty of their art — their weaving, baskets, pottery and beadwork. I had no idea that one day I would have the privilege of becoming a collector of such items — a temporary, loving caretaker until they are passed on from me to the next caretaker.

I acquired my first American Indian objects in a most unusual way. In 1960 I purchased an automobile from a ninety-year-old woman whose husband had died. She had never learned to drive, and sold me the car for the grand total of one hundred dollars. I drove the car home and opened the trunk to check the condition of the spare tire. To my surprise, inside the trunk were four beautiful American Indian baskets! I immediately returned to her home with baskets in hand and knocked on the door. She looked at the baskets and said, "Oh, my dear! I remember when we acquired these baskets. We were married when I was nineteen years old, and for our honeymoon we rode across the West by train and purchased American Indian items all along the way. I have no idea how these wound up in the trunk of this car, but you purchased the car and the baskets were in there, so they are yours." I protested! She insisted! And so my collection began.

In 1976 I was introduced to the world of the Arts and Crafts Movement by my friend Ferris, a remarkable architect. She knew of my passion for Frank Lloyd Wright and wanted to expand my knowledge of his era. She took me to the Gamble House in Pasadena, California, one of the most beautiful homes I have ever seen, and designed by the incredible Greene brothers. I wanted to obtain more information, but it was scarce. Thank goodness for Randell Makinson's two invaluable books that were published in the late 1970s, *Greene and Greene Architecture as a Fine Art* and *Greene and Greene Furniture and Related Design*. As I learned more about the Movement, I became fascinated with all the structures involved and all the different craftsmen and women in so many fields. Gustav Stickley, Charles Limbert, L. and J. G. Stickley (furniture); Arequipa, Grueby, Marblehead, Newcomb, Rookwood (pottery); Dirk van Erp, Roycroft, Heintz (metalwork); Tiffany, Handel, Duffner and Kimberly, Dirk van Erp (lamps) — to name just a few in each category. I loved the fact that the different companies were from around this nation and that Native American items were appreciated and purchased from the Indians and placed among the furnishings.

As time went on I was introduced to California Impressionist paintings. I found it interesting that so many of these artists had studied in France and then came to California to paint because of the incredible light and beautiful landscapes. I look at these paintings not only with an appreciation for their beauty but with a realization of how historically important they are, for this is how California once looked before freeways, shopping malls and millions of homes.

This passion started with my interest in Frank Lloyd Wright, so it was natural that the first American Arts and Crafts furniture I purchased in 1982 were four Frank Lloyd Wright design-influenced dining chairs made by Charles Limbert. It became a challenge to me to try to find pieces made by different men and women in each field of furniture, pottery, metalwork, lamps and paintings, as well as Native American objects. I have a deep appreciation for the talent, skill and beauty each item embodies, and I feel blessed to have so much of our American history around me.

When I met Sidney, he had a sizeable collection of French and American Impressionist paintings. He became fascinated with my collection, and together we have added to it.

We hope that you will find the exhibition pleasurable and informative, and that it will take you back to a time of American history (1876-1916) when so many great craftsmen and women, artists, sculptors, writers and bookbinders, Native Americans, potters and metalworkers united to create the great American Arts and Crafts Movement.

Alexandra Sheldon

Arts and Crafts Movement

The Arts and Crafts Movement was conceived in Britain and Europe in the mid-nineteenth century and was a direct contradiction to the Industrial Revolution that had spread to Europe and America. It countered the mass-produced Victorian bric-a-brac whose variety and volume was made possible by assembly-line machinery with interchangeable parts. Emphasizing the value of everyday objects and hand-craftsmanship, and arguing for design reform, the Arts and Crafts Movement emphasized design dedicated to function and environment. Its harmony and ornament were derived from nature and were relevant to materials and form. The results were integrated with interior schemes, and Arts and Crafts as a style became a way of living. Possessing an enduring design philosophy and the therapeutic influence of beauty and creativity in society, it redefined craft as art and craftsmen as artists.

University of Oxford's first Slade Professor of Fine Art, John Ruskin (1819-1900), blamed the ills of society on the factory system and codified the anti-industrialist philosophy of the Movement. "Censuring the products of machinery as monotonous, uninspiring goods that disassociated their users from contact with human creativity, Ruskin crusaded for hand labor as an essential human right that preserved dignity and inventiveness in society."[1]

William Morris (1834-1896), an English writer, designer, manufacturer, publisher and politician, strove to translate Ruskin's theories into reality, and devoted himself to the cause of craft and social reform. He believed the unification of labor, organization and art would create a harmonious society in which beauty and practicality would be inseparable. He preached, "Have nothing in your houses that you do not know to be useful, or believe to be beautiful."

Ruskin and Morris emerged as missionaries of aesthetic taste and stimulated a revival of handcraftsmanship that would improve the quality of commercially manufactured products in Britain. Their aspirations that common people would benefit from a revival of honest, handmade objects were not realized—common people could not afford them. The machine was to have its day.

Departing from English philosophies, American proponents of the Arts and Crafts Movement successfully promoted the decorative arts through craftsmen. "The crafts in America were not elevated out of industry into the fine arts, but instead were adapted to industry...despite the fact that most products were actually hybrids made by various hands and machines."[2]

The Movement took hold in America because American manufacturers were not philosophically opposed to the use of machinery. They were free of a class structure that added political pressures like those associated with the leaders in British design. Moreover, Americans were successful in their efforts to mechanize their processes without sacrificing improved craftsmanship and design, which was paramount to artistically unified interior design. In fact, a remarkable variety of international expressions comprised the Arts and Crafts Movement of the late nineteenth and early twentieth centuries. From its seminal ideas in Britain, the Movement spread to the United States, evidencing its finest flowering in New York, New England, Chicago and most vividly in California.

Gustav Stickley (1857-1942) was the major American follower of the Arts and Crafts Movement, along with writer and publisher Elbert Hubbard (1856-1915) and architect Frank Lloyd Wright (1867-1959). Stickley disagreed with the extreme British anti-industrial viewpoint and adapted his working methods to the existing market. While his simple and practical styles met the Movement's requirements for pure, functional design, they also facilitated machine production. He employed no unnecessary adornments or artificial trimmings in his elegantly functional furniture, but decorated his pieces with heavy, cast and hammered hardware and visible mortise-and-tenon joinery. Such simplicity was key to the success of his mechanization efforts, permitting departure from the high costs of handcraftsmanship.

[1] Leslie Green Bowman, *American Arts & Crafts: Virtue in Design* (Los Angeles, California: Los Angeles County Museum of Art, 1990), p. 17.

[2] Ibid., p. 33.

The success of the majority of American Arts and Crafts furniture manufacturers focused on the handcrafted *look* in design by using labor-saving machinery. Stickley and his brothers were joined in their ventures by other craftsmen most notably Charles P. Limbert (1854-1923). They created a thriving market for affordable, artistically designed furniture whose accessibility to the middle class fostered an appreciation and awareness of efficient design, honesty in materials and beauty in proportion and line. Production struggled and suffered with the onset of World War I, however, and in 1915 Gustav Stickley — uncompromising to the end — suffered bankruptcy.

The powerful influence of the American Arts and Crafts Movement had reached California by the turn of the twentieth century. California architects and craftsmen embraced its concept, incorporating form, function and environmental cohesiveness into buildings, furniture, metal art and pottery.

While Stickley and Wright were the leaders of the American version of the Movement in the East and Midwest, seminal figures on the West Coast were the brothers Charles (1868-1957) and Henry (1870-1954) Greene of Pasadena, California. The Greenes' work in residential architecture, furniture, glass, tile, textiles and metal objects, and its integration into California's bungalows, provided models for other gifted artisans. California's contribution to the American Arts and Crafts Movement was developing quickly.

After the great San Francisco earthquake and fire of 1906, production of crafts flourished. The massive rebuilding of the city encouraged a market for architecture, furniture and accessories. Bernard Maybeck (1862-1957) and Julia Morgan (1872-1957) became the most noted Northern California Arts and Crafts architects. Noted landscape painters and respected designers Arthur Mathews (1860-1945) and his wife Lucia Kleinhans Mathews (1870-1955) supplied paintings, furniture, picture frames and decorative objects to the rebuilt homes of the wealthy. The Mathewses developed their own style, termed the California Decorative Style, that demonstrated a strong affinity with the larger parent movement. Unlike purists in the American Arts and Crafts Movement who based beauty on sound structural qualities and the innate qualities of the materials, the Mathewses and other California talents did not disparage ornamentation. They cultivated their own well-defined regional market.

Paintings also found a special home in California, where landscapes reflected the tonal atmosphere of the San Francisco Bay Area or the Impressionist color and light of Southern California. They integrated well into California craftsman dwellings.

California was also rich in the output of ceramics and metal art during this period. Ceramics were especially strong, and a number of potteries were scattered throughout the state. Architectural tiles made by designers such as Ernest Batchelder (1875-1957), who worked in Pasadena and Los Angeles, were in great demand. Artistic metalwork flourished in San Francisco with the opening of numerous small workshops. Dirk van Erp (1860-1933) was California's most notable coppersmith, best known for copper lamps with mica shades that generated candle-like luminosity. The presence of hammer marks on metalwork announced craftsmanship even though machinery and other industrialized methods were employed.

The artistic value of most objects of the American Arts and Crafts Movement lies in the handcrafted design of the piece rather than in the manner in which it was made. While the Movement strived to preserve the handcrafted aspect of handmade objects and was "philosophically opposed to industrialization, the markets and methods of the industrial system enabled it to flourish in America more than in the country of its birth, England."[3]   *K.P.H.*

[3]Ibid., p. 42.

Furniture

The Sheldons have focused their furniture collecting on pieces by Gustav Stickley, the Stickley brothers and Charles P. Limbert.

In 1899 Gustav Stickley established United Crafts in Eastwood, New York, to make furniture that reflected expert craftsman's preoccupation with structure and materials. After a visit to England in 1898, Stickley followed the British arts and crafts philosophies of art and labor while adapting its theories to the American industry and market. Through the products of Stickley's workshops and in his influential monthly journal *The Craftsman* (in publication from 1901 until 1916), he promoted the new style throughout America.

Stickley moved beyond the British styles in 1903 by hiring architect Harvey Ellis (1852-1904) to provide new designs. His influence on Stickley's furniture revealed elongated and lightened pieces with taller proportions, thinner boards, broad overhangs, and arching skirts. He used ornament of inlays of stylized floral patterns in pewter, copper, and colored woods. "However elegant, Ellis's labor-intensive designs were expensive, and production never exceeded the promotional needs of retailers and expositions."[4] Stickley's business expanded to include metalwork accessories, lighting and textiles, and in 1904 he changed the business name to Gustav Stickley's Craftsman Workshops.

Branching out from his deliberately overconstructed pieces that suggested medieval and pre-Raphaelite influences, Stickley introduced slimmer, more attenuated "spindle" furniture from 1905 until about 1909, a design that was influenced by the spindle furniture of Frank Lloyd Wright of the late 1890s. After his stark and simple styles were copied and sold by other furniture manufacturers, Gustav Stickley's Craftsman Workshops lost clients, and Gustav declared bankruptcy in 1915.

In 1881, eight years before Gustav's business was established, two of his brothers, Albert (1863-1928) and John George (1871-1921), had operated the Stickley Brothers Company in Grand Rapids, Michigan, although Gustav's furniture bore no resemblance to that of his brothers. In response to Gustav's designs, however, brothers Albert and John George had introduced the Quaint line around 1900, which was followed by a line of inlaid furniture a year later. In 1902 John George collaborated with another brother, Leopold, who had previously worked with Gustav as a foreman. They established Onondaga Shops in Fayetteville, New York, until 1910, when the name was changed to L. and J. G. Stickley.

L. and J. G. Stickley aggressively merchandised their products to a larger audience, modeling their designs on the example of Gustav's company. When the popularity of American Arts and Crafts furniture diminished in the mid-teens, the Stickleys shifted their production to colonial revival styles. They took over Gustav's workshops in 1918, three years after the bankruptcy. Of the complex and sometimes simultaneous network of furniture manufacturing by the Stickley brothers, only L. and J. G. Stickley remains in operation today.

The Stickleys were joined in the design reform by numerous other furniture manufacturers. Among the most notable and superlative designs represented in the Sheldon collection are those of the Charles P. Limbert Company, which operated from the furniture mecca of Grand Rapids, Michigan. Founder Limbert produced quality furniture using fine materials and construction, taking advantage of mass production methods for prescribed designs. In 1906 he relocated his factory to Holland, Michigan, to a scenic lakeside location where workers experienced healthful and pleasant working conditions. Designers were given freedom to focus on visual effects and drew inspiration from British, Austrian and Japanese designs. The firm became notable for incorporating cutouts in a number of its pieces and for its use of parallel planes and pierced rectangles in the cross braces.   *K.P.H.*

[4]Ibid., p. 72.

Barber Brothers Chair Company,
Grand Rapids, Michigan,
ca. 1900-1911
SPINDLE TABORETS, pair
oak
h: 26; w: 13¼; d: 13¼ inches
catalog no. 1

Come-Packt Furniture
Company, Toledo, Ohio
SPINDLE SETTLE. 1912-1913
oak, leather
h: 29⅞; w: 69½; d: 25¾ inches
catalog no. 2

Greene and Greene, Pasadena,
California, 1893-1922
FRAME
oak, mirror
h: 18¼; w: 13; d: ¾ inches
catalog no. 3

catalog no. 7

Life Time Furniture, Grand
Rapids, Michigan
COSTUMER. ca. 1910
oak, metal hooks
h: 66¾; w: 18; d: 18 inches
catalog no. 4

Charles P. Limbert Company,
Grand Rapids and Holland,
Michigan, 1902-1944
CHINA CABINET
oak, glass
h: 61; w: 34¼; d: 16 inches
catalog no. 5

Charles P. Limbert Company,
Grand Rapids and Holland,
Michigan, 1902-1944
CUTOUT TABORET
oak
h: 18; w: 14 ¾; d: 14 ¾ inches
catalog no. 6

Charles P. Limbert Company,
Grand Rapids and Holland,
Michigan, 1902-1944
CUTOUT DROP FRONT DESK
WITH SIDE SHELVES
oak
h: 48 ½; w: 33 ½; d: 12 ½
inches
catalog no. 7

Charles P. Limbert Company,
Grand Rapids and Holland,
Michigan, 1902-1944
DINING TABLE WITH TWO
LEAVES
oak
h: 29; dia: 48 inches
catalog no. 8

Charles P. Limbert Company,
Grand Rapids and Holland,
Michigan, 1902-1944
DRINK STAND
oak
h: 26; w: 16; d: 16 inches
catalog no. 9

catalog no. 9

Charles P. Limbert Company,
Grand Rapids and Holland,
Michigan, 1902-1944
INLAID CHAIRS, PAIR
oak
h: 39 ¾; w: 25 ½; d: 23 inches
catalog no. 10

catalog no. 10

Charles P. Limbert Company,
Grand Rapids and Holland,
Michigan, 1902-1944
MIRROR
oak, mirror, brass hooks
h: 23 ½; w: 41 ¼; d: 1 ¼ inches
catalog no. 11

catalog no. 11

Charles P. Limbert Company,
Grand Rapids and Holland,
Michigan, 1902-1944
OVAL TABLE. ca. 1905-1910
oak
h: 29 ¼; w: 47 ½; d: 36 ¼
inches
catalog no. 12

Charles P. Limbert Company,
Grand Rapids and Holland,
Michigan, 1902-1944
SPINDLE DINING CHAIRS, FOUR.
ca. 1906
oak, leather
h: 38 ¼; w: 18; d: 17 ¼ inches
catalog no. 13

catalog no. 13

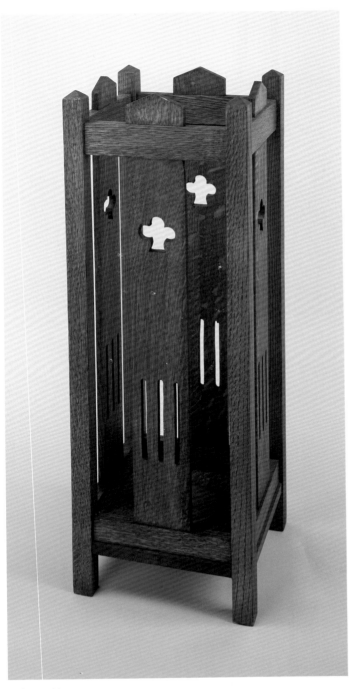

Charles P. Limbert Company,
Grand Rapids and Holland,
Michigan, 1902-1944
UMBRELLA STAND
oak
h: 32; w: 11; d: 11 inches
catalog no. 14

Gustav Stickley's Craftsman
Workshops, Eastwood and New
York, New York, 1899-1916
BOOKCASE
oak, glass, bronze hardware
h: 43 ¾; w: 39; d: 12 inches
catalog no. 15

Gustav Stickley's Craftsman
Workshops, Eastwood and New
York, New York, 1899-1916
LADY'S MORRIS CHAIR
oak, leather
h: 38 ¼; w: 27 ¾ d: 34 ⅜
inches
catalog no. 16

catalog no. 14

catalog no. 16

Gustav Stickley's Craftsman Workshops, Eastwood and New York, New York, 1899-1916
MAGAZINE STAND
oak
h: 42; w: 21 ½; d: 12 ¾ inches
catalog no. 17

Gustav Stickley's Craftsman Workshops, Eastwood and New York, New York, 1899-1916
PLANT STAND
oak
h: 28; w: 14 ½; d: 14 ⅞ inches
catalog no. 18

Gustav Stickley's Craftsman Workshops, Eastwood and New York, New York, 1899-1916
PLANT STAND
oak
h: 28; w: 14 ¾; d: 14 ¾ inches
catalog no. 19

Gustav Stickley's Craftsman Workshops, Eastwood and New York, New York, 1899-1916
SCRAP BASKET
oak, wrought iron hoops
h: 14; dia: 12 inches
catalog no. 20

Gustav Stickley's Craftsman Workshops, Eastwood and New York, New York, 1899-1916
SEWING TABLE
oak
h: 27 ⅞; w: 17 ¼; (w: 40 ¼ with leaves open) d: 16 ½ inches
catalog no. 21

Gustav Stickley's Craftsman Workshops, Eastwood and New York, New York, 1899-1916
SPINDLE FOOTSTOOL
oak, leather
h: 16; w: 17 ¾; d: 12 ¾ inches
catalog no. 22

catalog no. 17

catalog no. 18

Gustav Stickley's Craftsman
Workshops, Eastwood and New
York, New York, 1899-1916
Spindle Library Table
oak
h: 28 ⅝; w: 48 ¼; d: 29 ¾
inches
catalog no. 23

catalog no. 23

Gustav Stickley's Craftsman Workshops, Eastwood and New York, New York, 1899-1916
SPINDLE CHAIR
oak, leather
h: 37 ⅜; w: 18; d: 16 ¼ inches
catalog no. 24

Gustav Stickley's Craftsman Workshops, Eastwood and New York, New York, 1899-1916, and Grueby Faience Company, Boston, Massachusetts, 1894-1920
STICKLEY TABORET WITH ONE GRUEBY TILE
oak, glazed ceramic
h: 21; w: 16; d: 16 inches
catalog no. 25

Gustav Stickley's Craftsman Workshops, Eastwood and New York, New York, 1899-1916, and Grueby Faience Company, Boston, Massachusetts, 1894-1920
STICKLEY TEA TABLE WITH TWELVE GRUEBY TILES
oak, glazed ceramic
h: 25 ¾; w: 24; d: 20 ½ inches
catalog no. 26

L. and J. G. Stickley Furniture Company, Fayetteville, New York, 1902-present
SIDEBOARD
oak, hand-hammered copper hardware
h: 46; w: 56; d: 22 inches
catalog no. 27

L. and J. G. Stickley Furniture Company, Fayetteville, New York, 1902-present
SPINDLE CHAIR
oak, leather
h: 36½; w: 16¼; d: 14¼ inches
catalog no. 28

Stickley Brothers Company, Binghampton, New York, 1884-1890
Charles Stickley (1865-1928)
DAY BED
oak, leather
h: 28½; l: 75¼; w: 29 inches
catalog no. 29

Stickley Brothers Company, Grand Rapids, Michigan, 1891-1954
CHEST OF DRAWERS
oak
h: 47; w: 36; d: 21 inches
catalog no. 30

Stickley Brothers Company, Grand Rapids, Michigan, 1891-1954
SPINDLE BOW ARM CHAIR
oak, leather
h: 40; w: 31¼; d: 32 inches
catalog no. 31

Louis C. Tiffany & Co., Associated Artists, New York, New York, 1879-1885
FIRESCREEN. 1881
wood, glass tiles
h: 40; w: 25½; d: 16 inches
catalog no. 32

catalog no. 31

Metalwork and Lamps

The Sheldon collection of metalwork and lamps includes objects made by the masters of the furniture makers—Gustav Stickley's Craftsman Workshops, the Roycrofters and Charles P. Limbert Company—who followed the arts and crafts philosophy that home accessories should be useful, beautiful and an integral component of the environment. Metalwork and lamps became a popular means of artistic expression and were prolifically produced by many studios.

Gustav Stickley founded his metalworking shop to produce hardware that had the same structural and simple qualities as his furniture. Expanded to include accessories in copper and wrought iron, Stickley's metalwork is characteristically handcrafted, with obvious hammer marks and repoussé designs of simple and stylized floral patterns derived from English designs.

Shreve and Company, founded in 1852 in San Francisco, was a well-established silver manufacturer by the late nineteenth century. They responded to the Arts and Crafts Movement with special "handcrafted" designs. Hammer marks on most of the wares were added by hand after the form had been spun on a lathe, a typical mechanized compromise in American Arts and Crafts silver.

Heintz Art Metal Shop was established in 1905 in Buffalo, New York, by Otto L. Heintz. For twenty-four years the shop produced distinctive decorative accessories in bronze with sterling silver overlays. The handmade quality of the silver overlay melting, and the bonding to bronze surfaces, appealed to the Arts and Crafts sensibilities. Copper became a favored metal not only because of its more humble status but also because it was softer and could be worked more quickly than silver.

Around 1903 Elbert Hubbard established an art copper department in his Roycrofters workshops. He continued uninterrupted production until 1938, making hand-hammered copper vases, trays, bowls, candlesticks, lighting fixtures and other functional objects. Many Roycroft copperware designs were stamped with borders to emulate leather stitching. Former bookbinder Karl E. Kipp (1882-1954) was in charge of production from 1908 until 1911.

In 1908 Dirk van Erp opened the Copper Shop in Oakland, California, moving it to San Francisco when he took Elizabeth D'Arcy Gaw (1868-1944) as a design partner in 1910. Although she left the business after only a year, she is credited with introducing the more sophisticated designs. Van Erp's particular areas of expertise were in metalworking, hammering and the application of subtle patinas.

While producing a variety of accessories in copper, but also in brass and iron, van Erp's major contribution to the field was popularizing the use of mica in the shades of his copper lamps. With electric lighting, lamps with luminous mica lampshades provided a soft amber glow similar to candle illumination.

Another copper shop was established by Hans W. Jauchen (1863-1970) and Fred T. Brosi (d.1935) in the early 1920s, with a manufacturing plant in San Jose and a showroom in San Francisco. Old Mission Kopperkraft used various machines and molds to stamp out hammer patterns on copper designs similar to those of Dirk van Erp's studio.

Louis Comfort Tiffany (1848-1933), son of Charles Tiffany (owner of New York's Fifth Avenue Tiffany and Company), encouraged craftsmen to experiment and assist in the design process. Tiffany Studios was established in 1902 in Corona, New York, as a foundry to supply fittings and bases for the glass company. Tiffany's *Favrile* glass (a term coined by Tiffany to apply to all objects produced under his direct supervision), introduced in 1893, was often combined with metalwork to create lamps and other decorative objects. Among the most successful products of the firm were lamps, desk sets, candlesticks, metalwares, enamels and pottery, as well as cut glass. *K.P.H.*

Duffner and Kimberly, New
York, New York, 1906-1911
TABLE LAMP
bronze base; slag glass with
leaded flower design shade
h: 24½; dia: 18¾ inches
catalog no. 33

Duffner and Kimberly, New
York, New York, 1906-1911
TABLE LAMP
bronze base; slag glass with
leaded flower design shade
h: 23½; dia: 20 inches
catalog no. 34

The Handel Company, Meriden,
Connecticut
TABLE LAMP
bronze base; glass with bronze
overlay tree design shade
h: 25; w: 15¾; d: 15¾ inches
catalog no. 35

Heintz Art Metal Shop, Buffalo,
New York, 1906-1929
VASE
bronze with sterling silver leaf
overlay
h: 8¼; dia: 4¼ inches
catalog no. 36

Heintz Art Metal Shop, Buffalo,
New York, 1906-1929
VASE
bronze with sterling silver rose
overlay
h: 5; dia: 2⅞ inches
catalog no. 37

Heintz Art Metal Shop, Buffalo,
New York, 1906-1929
VASE
bronze with sterling silver
flower overlay
h: 6; dia: 4 inches
catalog no. 38

catalog no. 36 (left), catalog no. 37 (center), catalog no. 38 (right)

Jarvie Shop, Chicago, Illinois,
1904-ca. 1920
Robert Riddle Jarvie
(1865-1941)
CANDLESTICKS, pair
bronze
h: 11; dia: 4½ inches
catalog no. 39

Charles P. Limbert Company,
Grand Rapids and Holland,
Michigan, 1902-1944
TABLE LAMP
hand-hammered copper base;
slag glass with copper overlay
shade
h: 22; dia: 25 inches
catalog no. 40

Charles P. Limbert Company,
Grand Rapids and Holland,
Michigan, 1902-1944
TABLE LAMP
hand-hammered copper base;
mica with copper overlay
hanging grape design shade
h: 25; w: 21; d: 21 inches
catalog no. 41

catalog no. 41

Old Mission Kopperkraft, San
Jose and San Francisco,
California, 1922-ca. 1925
BOOKENDS, pair
hand-hammered copper
h: 5¼; w: 5; d: 3¾ inches
catalog no. 42

Old Mission Kopperkraft, San
Jose and San Francisco,
California, 1922-ca. 1925
TABLE LAMP
hand-hammered copper base;
mica shade
h: 15; dia: 19 inches
catalog no. 43

Quezal Art Glass and
Decorating Company, Brooklyn,
New York
THREE-LIGHT LILY TABLE LAMP
copper base; glass shades
h: 11¾; w: 12; d: 12 inches
catalog no. 44

The Roycrofters Copper Shop,
East Aurora, New York,
ca. 1903-1938
BOOKENDS, pair
hand-hammered copper
h: 8½; w: 5¾; d: 3¾ inches
catalog no. 45

The Roycrofters Copper Shop,
East Aurora, New York,
ca. 1903-1938
BOWL
hand-hammered copper
h: 4; dia: 10 inches
catalog no. 46

catalog no. 44

catalog no. 49

The Roycrofters Copper Shop,
East Aurora, New York,
ca. 1903-1938
BOWL
hand-hammered copper
h: 3; dia: 9 inches
catalog no. 47

The Roycrofters Copper Shop,
East Aurora, New York,
ca. 1903-1938
VASE
hand-hammered copper
h: 4; dia: 6½ inches
catalog no. 48

The Roycrofters Copper Shop,
East Aurora, New York,
ca. 1903-1938
VASE
hand-hammered copper with
silver overlay
h: 6¼; dia: 3 inches
catalog no. 49

Shreve and Company,
San Francisco, California,
1852-present
SILVER FLATWARE
silver
various patterns and dimensions
catalog no. 50

catalog no. 50

Gustav Stickley's Craftsman
Workshops, Eastwood and New
York, New York, 1899-1916
CANDLESTICK. 1913-1915
hand-hammered copper
h: 9; dia: 7⅛ inches
catalog no. 51

catalog no. 51

Tiffany Studios, Corona and
New York, New York,
1902-1938
DESK SET
Favrile glass and etched metal
inkwell: h: 3½; w: 4¼; d: 4¼;
letter holder: h: 8½; l: 12½;
d: 3½; pencil holder: h: 1½;
l: 8½; d: 3; frame: h: 7¼;
w: 8¾ inches
catalog no. 52

Tiffany Studios, Corona and
New York, New York,
1902-1938, and
Buffalo Studios, Santa Ana,
California, 1972-present
TIFFANY FLOOR LAMP BASE
WITH BUFFALO STUDIOS
REPRODUCTION SHADE
bronze base; slag glass with
leaded spider design shade
h: 53½; dia: 15 inches
catalog no. 53

catalog no. 52

catalog no. 54

Tiffany Studios, Corona and
New York, New York,
1902-1938
POPPY LIBRARY LAMP
bronze lily stem design base;
leaded glass poppy design shade
h: 25½; dia: 20¼ inches
catalog no. 54

Tiffany Studios, Corona and
New York, New York,
1902-1938
READING LAMP
Favrile blown glass base and
shade
h: 14; dia: 7¼ inches
catalog no. 55

Tiffany Studios, Corona and
New York, New York,
1902-1938
PICTURE FRAME
Favrile glass with etched metal
h: 10; w: 8 inches
catalog no. 56

Tiffany Studios, Corona and
New York, New York,
1902-1938
TORCHIERES, pair
bronze bases; Favrile blown
glass shades
h: 22¾; dia: 6½ inches
catalog no. 57

Dirk van Erp Copper Shop,
Oakland and San Francisco,
California, 1908-1977
BOUDOIR LAMP
hand-hammered copper base;
mica and copper shade
h: 10¾; dia: 11¼ inches
catalog no. 58

Dirk van Erp Copper Shop,
Oakland and San Francisco,
California, 1908-1977
BOWL
hand-hammered copper with
pronounced wart-like finish
h: 5¾; dia: 6½ inches
catalog no. 59

Dirk van Erp Copper Shop,
Oakland and San Francisco,
California, 1908-1977
BOWL
hand-hammered copper
h: 4⅞; dia: 5¼ inches
catalog no. 60

Dirk van Erp Copper Shop,
Oakland and San Francisco,
California, 1908-1977
CLOCK
brass
h: 4¾; w: 3½; d: 1 inches
catalog no. 61

Dirk van Erp Copper Shop,
Oakland and San Francisco,
California, 1908-1977
FLOOR ASHTRAY ON SPINDLE
STAND
hand-hammered copper
h: 31; dia: 8 inches
catalog no. 62

Dirk van Erp Copper Shop,
Oakland and San Francisco,
California, 1908-1977
FLOOR LAMP. ca. 1915
hand-hammered copper base;
mica and copper swivel shade
h: 59½; w: 21; d: 11½ inches
catalog no. 63

Dirk van Erp Copper Shop,
Oakland and San Francisco,
California, 1908-1977
TABLE LAMP. ca. 1912
hand-hammered copper base;
mica and copper shade
h: 20¾; dia: 20¼ inches
catalog no. 64

Dirk van Erp Copper Shop,
Oakland and San Francisco,
California, 1908-1977
VASE
hand-hammered copper
h: 7; dia: 5 inches
catalog no. 65

Wheatley Pottery Company,
Cincinnati, Ohio, 1903-1927,
and
The Handel Company, Meriden,
Connecticut
WHEATLEY TABLE LAMP BASE
WITH HANDEL SHADE
pottery base; leaded glass shade
h: 21½; dia: 16¾ inches
catalog no. 66

Ceramics

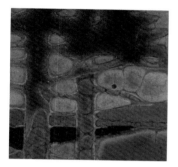

The Sheldons' selection of American pottery is a nationally focused collection with a strong interest in California pottery. They have collected art pottery made by such large studios as Rookwood, Weller, Newcomb, Grueby and Fulper, as well as works by smaller workshops including Hampshire, Marblehead and Arequipa. American firms produced quality objects intended for a commercial market while facing the dilemma of reform as espoused by the original Arts and Crafts Movement. Concerned with producing pottery of aesthetic integrity and educating public taste, they also were interested in profits. Many produced less expensive commercial lines whose proceeds assured the continuation of artistic production.

Among the largest potteries in the country during the 1910s were Weller, Rookwood and Grueby. S. A. Weller Pottery became the leader in mass-produced, low-priced art pottery. The most artistic ceramics produced at Weller were designed by Frederick H. Rhead (1880-1942) and Jacques Sicard (1865-1923). In four decades, Rhead left his mark on the ceramic production of numerous other major potteries in the United States, including Roseville, University City, Arequipa, American Encaustic and others.

Inspired by the popularity of Tiffany's glass, Weller hired French ceramicist Jacques Sicard in 1901 to develop a metallic lusterware. Influenced by the work of his former employer Clément Massier, and working in secrecy for two years to protect the newly developed formula, Sicard produced an iridescent pottery for Weller, which was known as "Sicardo."

Founded in 1880 specifically for constructing and decorating art pottery by hand, Rookwood Pottery was one of the earliest and most influential art potteries. Unlike commercial firms that produced art ceramics as a sideline, Rookwood's production was characterized by a variety of styles, shapes and techniques of decoration, and its success was partially the result of the firm's adaptability to changing tastes. Japanese ceramicist Kataro Shirayamadani (1865-1948) joined the firm in 1887 and quickly became one of the company's principal designers, remaining at Rookwood until his death.

Grueby Faience Company became one of the largest producers of architectural brick and tile, and is credited with the 1897 introduction of an innovative matte green glaze. The appeal of the Grueby glaze was its rich, monotone, matte surface. Under the name Grueby Pottery, which was established in 1907 to produce art wares only, the adaptation of handicraft techniques to mass production removed creative decision making from the technician. Patterns became standardized. The vessels were hand-constructed by men, and women decorated the pieces with established designs. Many of the craftspeople were art students. Grueby's use of traditional hand-production methods, combined with the division of labor associated with industry, was much admired by proponents of the American Arts and Crafts Movement.

The Fulper Pottery Company had been established as a commercial operation years before its line of artware was first produced. In 1909 "Vasekraft" was introduced to supply the middle class with a relatively inexpensive, well-made art pottery. Pieces were cast in molds, then individually glazed by hand. Fulper became known for the wide range of glaze effects that could be achieved by combining or overlapping different glazes on the same piece.

James Robertson established the Chelsea Keramic Art Works in 1872 with his sons, Alexander and Hugh. Notable among the Robertsons' smooth, fine-textured wares was a group of classically inspired vases. Pieces were often decorated with applied carved sprigs of flowers, leaves, birds or bees. At his father's death in 1880 and Alexander's move to California in 1884, Hugh C. Robertson remained as sole owner of the company. Abandoning the elaborate decorative format, Robertson turned to the Oriental style, adapting the Japanese crackle glaze that later became the specialty of Dedham Pottery. In 1896 Chelsea Keramic Art Works was renamed Dedham Pottery, and its most popular products were the crackleware dinner services made in a variety of floral and animal patterns of many colors.

Teco was the ceramics line of Gates Potteries, a subsidiary of American Terra Cotta and Ceramic Company. The Teco line was introduced in 1900 to produce art pottery from molded rather than handmade forms at a reasonable price, and it capitalized on the popularity of the newly developed matte green glaze. Teco depended upon simple form and color rather than surface decoration. Many vessels were designed by young Chicago architects representing the Prairie School, including Frank Lloyd Wright. The resulting forms are distinguished by their stylized geometric, architectonic and monumental elements.

Working alone, Charles Walter Clewell (1876-1965) was responsible for developing a category of art pottery using a unique metal coating on pottery blanks. He developed a process of applying a thin skin of bronze or copper to the ceramic form, which simulated metalwork. He also developed techniques to adhere metal to clay, allowing oxidation that produced various surface colorations. Later Clewell's experiments led to chemical treatments of metal coatings to attain the blue-green patinated effect for which he became well known.

Founded in 1895, Newcomb Pottery was an educational enterprise associated with Sophie Newcomb Memorial College in New Orleans, Louisiana. Newcomb employed men to throw pots by hand, trained young women in the marketable and respectable skill of pottery decoration and hired graduates of the college to produce saleable goods.

Marblehead, Paul Revere and Arequipa Potteries were founded on the basis of social and commercial purposes. Marblehead Pottery was established in 1904 as a workshop to provide therapy for convalescing patients. It soon achieved independent commercial success with simple forms decorated with subtly colored matte glazes. Following the tradition of Grueby, Marblehead specialized in soft matte glazes and stylized naturalistic designs, which were either incised or painted. In contrast to Grueby, Marblehead abstracted natural motifs instead of imitating them.

The social mission of the American Arts and Crafts Movement also found expression at the Paul Revere Pottery, which established a Saturday Evening Girls' Club as a cultural and social organization to provide young Jewish and Italian immigrant women with training in pottery throwing, design and glaze chemistry.

Arequipa (Peruvian for "place of rest") Pottery was established as a sanatorium for tubercular women. Organized by noted ceramicist Frederick Hurten Rhead, men were hired to throw or mold vessels, and patients were trained in decorating and glazing. Vases were often decorated with a design process he called the "raised line," in which slip was trailed onto vessels in decorative patterns and accentuated by other glazes. A stylized organic design of meandering leaves evidences Rhead's English arts and crafts training. After leaving Arequipa in 1913, Rhead remained in California and founded his own pottery workshop in 1914 in Santa Barbara.

Ernest Allan Batchelder (1875-1957) was a leading tile designer of the American Arts and Crafts Movement, already well known when he founded his own tile company in Pasadena in 1909. Southern California's booming construction industry called for architectural tiles, fireplaces, fountains and other architectural elements. Batchelder continued to maintain the craftsman ethic of handmade products, molding tiles in plaster molds then decorating them with unique glazes. Batchelder abided by his own precepts of ordered design achieved through harmony, balance and rhythm. Medieval motifs and Mediterranean and Mayan subjects influenced his designs as well.

Grand Feu Art Pottery was established in 1913 to produce a ceramic ware that imitated porcelain with technically sophisticated glazes. Grand Feu used applied or painted decorations relying on the play of colors harmoniously blended by glazing and firing effects for their originality.

California Faience Company was founded around 1915 and became one of the most prolific and successful California art potteries. California Faience made economical use of molds and, with few exceptions, limited decoration on vessels to glazes only, ranging from brilliant high-gloss hues to subtle matte surfaces. Reliance on aesthetically pleasing form and glaze eliminated the need for expensive hand decoration. *K.P.H.*

Arequipa Pottery, Fairfax,
California, 1911-1918
BOWL
ceramic, dark blue matte glaze
with green leaf pattern
h: 2⅝; dia: 7 inches
catalog no. 67

Arequipa Pottery, Fairfax,
California, 1911-1918
VASE. 1913
ceramic, matte green glaze,
"squeeze-bag" raised leaf design
h: 6; dia: 3¾ inches
catalog no. 68

Arequipa Pottery, Fairfax,
California, 1911-1918
VASE
ceramic, light blue glaze with
raised flower design
h: 7; dia: 4 inches
catalog no. 69

Arequipa Pottery, Fairfax,
California, 1911-1918
BOWL. 1911-1912
ceramic, dark green matte glaze
with incised flower pattern
h: 2⅛; dia: 5⅝ inches
catalog no. 70

catalog no. 68 (left), catalog no. 72 (right)

Arequipa Pottery, Fairfax,
California, 1911-1918
VASE
ceramic, matte light green
glaze, crackle finish with incised
flowers and leaves
h: 5¼; dia: 4¼ inches
catalog no. 71

Arequipa Pottery, Fairfax,
California, 1911-1918
VASE. 1913
ceramic, brown matte glaze
with "squeeze-bag" raised flower
design
h: 7⅜; dia: 4 inches
catalog no. 72

Batchelder Tile Company,
Pasadena and Los Angeles,
California, 1909-1932
TILE FIREPLACE SURROUND.
ca. 1910
ceramic
h: 50¼; w: 56; d: 23 inches
catalog no. 73

Batchelder Tile Company,
Pasadena and Los Angeles,
California, 1909-1932
SCENIC TILE. ca. 1910
ceramic with falcon pattern
h: 3⅞; w: 3⅞; d: ¾ inches
catalog no. 74

Batchelder Tile Company,
Pasadena and Los Angeles,
California, 1909-1932
SCENIC TILE. ca. 1910
ceramic with castle and tree
pattern
h: 3⅞; w: 3⅞; d: ¾ inches
catalog no. 75

Biloxi Art Pottery, Biloxi,
Mississippi, 1883-1906
George Edgar Ohr (1857-1918)
VASE
ceramic, brown glaze with
pinched top
h: 3¾; dia: 3⅝ inches
catalog no. 76

California Faience Company,
Berkeley, California, 1915-1930
EAGLE BOOKENDS, pair
ceramic, matte blue glaze
h: 6¼; w: 5¾; d: 3 inches
catalog no. 77

California Faience Company,
Berkeley, California, 1915-1930
VASE
ceramic, blue glaze with raised
flower design
h: 2⅜; dia: 3⅞ inches
catalog no. 78

Chelsea Keramic Art Works,
Chelsea, Massachusetts,
1872-1889,
(Robertson & Sons)
SQUARE-SHAPED VASE WITH
HANDLES
ceramic, matte gold glaze with
green flowers, birds and bees
pattern
h: 6¾; w: 3½; d: 2½ inches
catalog no. 79

Clewell Metal Art, Canton,
Ohio, 1906-1965
Charles Walter Clewell
(1876-1965)
COUGAR BOOKENDS, pair
copper sheath over ceramic,
matte green and copper glaze
h: 8; w: 7¼; d: 5¾ inches
catalog no. 80

catalog no. 76

catalog no. 71

catalog no. 79

Clewell Metal Art, Canton,
Ohio, 1906-1965
Charles Walter Clewell
(1876-1965)
VASE
copper sheath over ceramic,
matte green and copper glaze
h: 9⅝; dia: 5¼ inches
catalog no. 81

Clewell Metal Art, Canton,
Ohio, 1906-1965
Charles Walter Clewell
(1876-1965)
VASE
copper sheath over ceramic,
matte green and copper glaze
h: 9⅛; dia: 4⅜ inches
catalog no. 82

Clewell Metal Art, Canton,
Ohio, 1906-1965
Charles Walter Clewell
(1876-1965)
VASE
copper sheath over ceramic,
matte green and copper glaze
h: 4¼; dia: 3¼ inches
catalog no. 84

Clewell Metal Art, Canton,
Ohio, 1906-1965
Charles Walter Clewell
(1876-1965)
VASE
copper sheath over ceramic,
matte green and copper glaze
h: 6; dia: 3¼ inches
catalog no. 83

Clewell Metal Art, Canton,
Ohio, 1906-1965
Charles Walter Clewell
(1876-1965)
VASE
copper sheath over ceramic,
matte green and copper glaze
h: 5¼; dia: 4¾ inches
catalog no. 85

catalog no. 85 (far left), catalog no. 82 (left), catalog no. 81 (center), catalog no. 83 (right), catalog no. 84 (far right)

Dedham Pottery, Dedham,
Massachusetts, 1896-1943
Hugh Robertson (1844-1908)
VASE
ceramic, marbleized green glaze
h: 8; dia: 3 inches
catalog no. 86

Dedham Pottery, Dedham,
Massachusetts, 1896-1943
LILY PLATE
ceramic, white-crackled and
cobalt blue glaze
dia: 10 inches
catalog no. 87

catalog no. 87

Fulper Pottery Company,
Flemington, New Jersey, 1860-
ca. 1935
Narrow-necked Vase
ceramic, blue glaze with snake-
like design
h: 7¾; dia: 3¾ inches
catalog no. 88

Fulper Pottery Company,
Flemington, New Jersey, 1860-
ca. 1935
Vase
ceramic, green flambé over
matte glaze
h: 3¾; dia: 10¼ inches
catalog no. 89

Fulper Pottery Company,
Flemington, New Jersey, 1860-
ca. 1935
Vase
ceramic, matte pink glaze
h: 5½; dia: 5 inches
catalog no. 90

Grand Feu Art Pottery,
Los Angeles, California,
ca. 1913-ca. 1916
Bowl
ceramic, tan and blue glaze
h: 1¾; dia: 5¾ inches
catalog no. 91

Grueby Faience Company,
Boston, Massachusetts,
1894-1920
Addison B. LeBoutillier
(1872-1951)
The Pines (one tile from a
frieze designed as a set of eight
tiles). ca. 1906-1920
ceramic, seven glazes, with
pines, lake and mountains
h: 6⅛; w: 6⅛; d: 1⅛ inches
catalog no. 92

Grueby Faience Company,
Boston, Massachusetts,
1894-1920
Scenic Tile
ceramic, matte glazes with
sailing ship design
h: 6¼; w: 6⅛; d: 1⅛ inches
catalog no. 93

Grueby Faience Company,
Boston, Massachusetts,
1894-1920
Scenic Tile
ceramic, matte glazes with
sailing ship design
h: 6¼; w: 6⅛; d: 1⅛ inches
catalog no. 94

catalog no. 90 (left), catalog no. 121 (center), catalog no. 125 (right)

Grueby Faience Company,
Boston, Massachusetts,
1894-1920
VASE
ceramic, matte green glaze with
raised flower buds
h: 8¼; dia. 5¼ inches
catalog no. 95

Grueby Pottery, Boston,
Massachusetts, 1907-1913
VASE
ceramic, matte green glaze with
raised flower buds
h: 8½; dia. 4⅝ inches
catalog no. 96

Grueby Pottery, Boston,
Massachusetts, 1907-1913
Gertrude Priest
VASE
ceramic, matte green glaze with
raised flower pattern
h: 10½; dia. 8¼ inches
catalog no. 97

Grueby Pottery, Boston,
Massachusetts, 1907-1913
VASE
ceramic, matte green glaze with
yellow raised flower buds
h: 6¾; dia. 4½ inches
catalog no. 98

Grueby Pottery, Boston,
Massachusetts, 1907-1913
VASE
ceramic, matte green glaze with
raised leaf design
h: 5⅝; dia: 6½ inches
catalog no. 99

Grueby Pottery, Boston,
Massachusetts, 1907-1913
VASE
ceramic, matte green glaze with
raised flower pattern
h: 11¼; dia: 5¾ inches
catalog no. 100

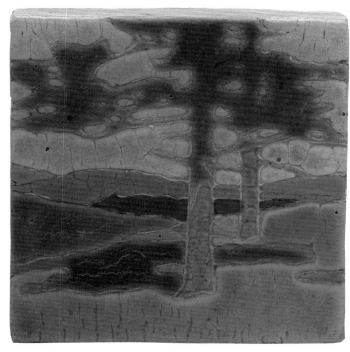

catalog no. 92

catalog no. 100

Hampshire Pottery, Keene, New Hampshire, 1871-1923
Cadmon Robertson
BOWL
ceramic, matte green glaze with raised water lily design
h: 3; dia: 10 inches
catalog no. 101

Marblehead Pottery, Marblehead, Massachusetts, 1904-1936
BOWL
ceramic, matte blue glaze with incised flower and leaf pattern
h: 3⅜; dia: 4½ inches
catalog no. 102

Marblehead Pottery, Marblehead, Massachusetts, 1904-1936
VASE
ceramic, grey glaze with blue flower design
h: 3½; dia: 4⅜ inches
catalog no. 103

Marblehead Pottery, Marblehead, Massachusetts, 1904-1936
VASE
ceramic, blue glaze with dark green and red tree design
h: 8⅞; dia: 5 inches
catalog no. 104

catalog no. 105 (left), catalog no. 104 (back), catalog no. 108 (front), catalog no. 150 (right)

Marblehead Pottery,
Marblehead, Massachusetts,
1904-1936
VASE
ceramic, pink glaze with blue
grape leaves design
h: 5½; dia: 3½ inches
catalog no. 105

Marblehead Pottery,
Marblehead, Massachusetts,
1904-1936
VASE
ceramic, matte blue glaze with
dark blue design
h: 5¼; dia: 3⅜ inches
catalog no. 106

Clément Massier Pottery, Golfe
Juan, France
Clément Massier (died 1917)
VASE
ceramic, iridescent purple and
gold glaze with lily pattern
h: 7¼; dia: 5⅜ inches
catalog no. 107

catalog no. 159 (left), catalog no. 107 (right)

Newcomb Pottery, New Orleans, Louisiana, 1895-1940
VASE
ceramic, green glaze with blue and pink flower design
h: 4⅝; dia: 2⅛ inches
catalog no. 108

Newcomb Pottery, New Orleans, Louisiana, 1895-1940
Sadie Irvine (1887-1970)
BOWL. 1910
ceramic, blue and green glaze with iris pattern
h: 6¾; dia: 8¾ inches
catalog no. 109

Newcomb Pottery, New Orleans, Louisiana, 1895-1940
Sadie Irvine (1887-1970)
VASE. 1921
ceramic, blue glaze with tan and green leaves and berries
h: 4⅜; dia: 3½ inches
catalog no. 110

Newcomb Pottery, New Orleans, Louisiana, 1895-1940
Sadie Irvine (1887-1970)
VASE. 1918
ceramic, blue and green glaze with trees and moon
h: 8¼; dia: 3⅝ inches
catalog no. 111

catalog no. 109

Rookwood Pottery, Cincinnati, Ohio, 1880-1960
Edward Timothy Hurley (1869-1950)
VASE. 1945
ceramic, scenic vellum woodland scene
h: 13; dia: 6½ inches
catalog no. 133

Rookwood Pottery, Cincinnati, Ohio, 1880-1960
Katherine Jones
VASE. 1923
ceramic, wax matte brown glaze with blue and pink floral design
h: 6⅝; dia: 7¾ inches
catalog no. 134

Rookwood Pottery, Cincinnati, Ohio, 1880-1960
William Purcell McDonald (1865-1931)
ELEPHANT BOOKENDS, pair. 1929
ceramic, green glaze
h: 7⅛; w: 5¼; d: 2¾ inches
catalog no. 135

Rookwood Pottery, Cincinnati, Ohio, 1880-1960
Mary Madeline Nourse (1870-1959)
VASE. 1892
ceramic, standard high gloss green glaze with sterling silver overlay
h: 6⅝; dia: 5⅛ inches
catalog no. 136

Rookwood Pottery, Cincinnati, Ohio, 1880-1960
Frederick Daniel Henry Rothenbush
VASE. 1925
ceramic, scenic vellum landscape
h: 11; dia: 5¾ inches
catalog no. 137

catalog no. 136 (left), catalog no. 157 (right)

Rookwood Pottery, Cincinnati,
Ohio, 1880-1960
Kataro Shirayamadani
(1865-1948)
VASE. 1938
ceramic, wax matte blue glaze
with green and ivory
hollyhocks
h: 10½; dia: 5¾ inches
catalog no. 138

Rookwood Pottery, Cincinnati,
Ohio, 1880-1960
Artus Van Briggle (1869-1904)
PITCHER
ceramic, standard high gloss
brown glaze with gold floral
design
h: 10¼; dia: 6¾ inches
catalog no. 139

Roseville Pottery, Zanesville,
Ohio, 1892-1954
VASE WITH HANDLES
(Carnelian II series). 1915
ceramic, matte pink and green
glaze
h: 12¼; dia: 7½ inches
catalog no. 140

catalog no. 139

catalog no. 138

catalog no. 140

Teco, Terra Cotta, Illinois,
ca. 1885-1941
(Gates Potteries)
VASE
ceramic, matte green glaze
h: 6½; dia: 5½ inches
catalog no. 141

Teco, Terra Cotta, Illinois,
ca. 1885-1941
(Gates Potteries)
VASE
ceramic, matte green glaze
h: 4⅜; dia: 4 inches
catalog no. 142

Van Briggle Pottery, Colorado
Springs, Colorado, 1902-present
BOWL. 1907
ceramic, matte green glaze with
raised pattern
h: 4½; dia: 5⅞ inches
catalog no. 143

Van Briggle Pottery, Colorado
Springs, Colorado, 1902-present
VASE. 1914
ceramic, matte green glaze with
raised flower pattern
h: 5⅜; dia: 3⅝ inches
catalog no. 144

Van Briggle Pottery, Colorado
Springs, Colorado, 1902-present
Artus Van Briggle (1869-1904)
VASE
ceramic, matte green glaze with
raised floral design
h: 9¾; dia: 3¾ inches
catalog no. 145

Volkmar Pottery, Corona, New
York, 1895-1911
Charles Volkmar (1841-1914)
BOWL
ceramic, green glaze
h: 3; dia: 7 inches
catalog no. 146

Volkmar Pottery, Corona, New
York, 1895-1911
Charles Volkmar (1841-1914)
VASE
ceramic, blue/green glaze with
raised design
h: 8¼; dia: 6½ inches
catalog no. 147

Walrath Pottery, Rochester, New
York, 1908-1918
CANDLESTICK
ceramic, brown glaze with flame
design
h: 6½; dia: 4¾ inches
catalog no. 148

Walrath Pottery, Rochester, New
York, 1908-1918
PITCHER WITH FOUR MATCHING
MUGS
ceramic, matte brown glaze
with green and brown pine cone
design
pitcher: h: 8¼; dia: 7¼;
mugs: h: 3⅝; dia: 4 inches
catalog no. 149

Walrath Pottery, Rochester, New
York, 1908-1918
VASE
ceramic, green glaze with gold
and dark green pine cone design
h: 8¼; dia: 4½ inches
catalog no. 150

S. A. Weller Pottery, Zanesville,
Ohio, 1872-1948
UMBRELLA STAND. ca. 1910
ceramic, matte green glaze with
raised flowers
h: 20½; dia: 10½ inches
catalog no. 151

S. A. Weller Pottery, Zanesville,
Ohio, 1872-1948
VASE
ceramic, matte green glaze with
white and yellow raised flower
design
h: 9½; dia: 5⅜ inches
catalog no. 152

S. A. Weller Pottery, Zanesville,
Ohio, 1872-1948
VASE. 1910
ceramic, matte green glaze with
flat leaf design
h: 9; dia: 11½ inches
catalog no. 153

S. A. Weller Pottery, Zanesville,
Ohio, 1872-1948
VASE (Velva ware). 1933
ceramic, matte blue glaze with
purple and green raised floral
design
h: 7¼; dia: 6½ inches
catalog no. 154

S. A. Weller Pottery, Zanesville,
Ohio, 1872-1948
VASE (Velva ware). 1933
ceramic, matte green glaze with
pink, white and brown raised
floral design
h: 5½; dia: 6⅛ inches
catalog no. 155

S. A. Weller Pottery, Zanesville,
Ohio, 1872-1948
VASE
ceramic, matte green glaze with
raised decoration
h: 9½; dia: 11½ inches
catalog no. 156

S. A. Weller Pottery, Zanesville,
Ohio, 1872-1948
Anna Dautherty
VASE (Louwelsa ware)
ceramic, high gloss brown glaze
with Indian Chief design
h: 11½; dia: 6¾ inches
catalog no. 157

S. A. Weller Pottery, Zanesville,
Ohio, 1872-1948
Jacques Sicard (1865-1923)
VASE (Sicardo ware).
ca. 1902-1907
ceramic, iridescent blue, purple
and gold glaze with iris pattern
h: 12; dia: 7⅛ inches
catalog no. 158

S. A. Weller Pottery, Zanesville,
Ohio, 1872-1948
Jacques Sicard (1865-1923)
VASE (Sicardo ware).
ca. 1902-1907
ceramic, iridescent green, gold
and purple glaze with snail
pattern
h: 12¼; dia: 5 inches
catalog no. 159

Paintings

Rooted in the social and aesthetic theories of John Ruskin and William Morris, the Arts and Crafts Movement announced that the integrity of design and craftsmanship were the basis of all good art. The stylistic basis of Arts and Crafts painting originated from the simplified, flat compositions of Japanese woodcuts and bold color of the French Post-Impressionists. Harvey Ellis, a designer for Gustav Stickley, was among those purists of the Movement who banned paintings from interiors because of their "stigma" as fine art rather than craft. While traditional paintings were often denied entry into proper craftsman dwellings, pictorial imagery found expression in pottery. Some Rookwood and Newcomb pottery was decorated with landscapes and decorative tiles, such as those by Addison B. LeBoutillier (1872-1951) who typically portrayed scenes with pine trees, lakes and mountains. Similar landscape reliefs appeared in Ernest Batchelder's tile work.

As the American Arts and Crafts Movement spread to the West Coast, California became the locale of the fullest expressions of its ideals. Painting also found a special home in California, where the landscape and the indigenous color and light combined with the craftsman ethos to create a regional style. In California the unpolluted and unpopulated landscapes of a vast new territory evoked an enormous range of creativity.

Arthur Mathews brought a form of Tonalism to Northern California at the turn of the century. He assimilated influences of the French academic style and an energizing European Modernism to produce the distinctive artistic components now recognized as the California Decorative Style.[5]

Tonalism became popular in Northern California where artists conveyed emotional and poetic sentiment in paintings of the San Francisco Bay Area. Giuseppe L. Cadenasso (1854-1918), Thomas A. McGlynn (1878-1966) and Gottardo F. P. Piazzoni (1872-1945) used Tonalism in their landscapes to depict atmospheric effects of morning mists, fogs and evening hues.

Outdoor painting became increasingly popular as artists were eager to document their painted responses to the California countryside, as in a private diary. Their on-the-spot impressions freshly interpreted their feelings about the transience of light and sky. This breed of painters spontaneously captured visual excitement, often by painting small canvases to swiftly capture the experience of direct observation.

The intimate dialogue between the artist and the landscape was developed by Impressionism, a radical movement in France in the 1870s. Post-Impressionism soon followed with a stronger use of pure color and simplified forms. By the turn of the century, Impressionism and Post-Impressionism were accepted and embraced by California artists who used the techniques and colorful palette to capture the state's distinctive topographical and atmospheric conditions.

While the hazy light of the Northern California landscape was appropriate to Tonalism, the brilliant sunshine and reflected light of the Southern California landscape as witnessed by Carl Oscar Borg (1879-1947), Maurice Braun (1877-1941), Charles A. Fries (1854-1940), William Lees Judson (1842-1928), Edgar A. Payne (1883-1947) and Elmer (1864-1929) and Marion Kavanaugh Wachtel (1876-1954) was ideally suited to Impressionism.

California artists developed a stronger use of form, color and texture than other American Impressionists, often combining other styles in a single work. Franz A. Bischoff (1864-1929), Granville Redmond (1871-1935) and William Wendt (1865-1946) were among artists who combined unlikely stylistic characteristics in their paintings. A new style of *en plein air* painting emerged, which complemented and found refuge in the American Arts and Crafts Movement.   *K.P.H.*

[5]Harvey L. Jones, *Mathews, Masterpieces of the California Decorative Style* (Layton, Utah: Gibbs M. Smith, Inc., 1985), p. 32.

Franz Arthur Bischoff
(1864-1929)
EUCALYPTUS LANDSCAPE WITH
HOUSE
oil on board
h: 13; w: 16½ inches
catalog no. 160

Franz Arthur Bischoff
(1864-1929)
MOUNTAIN LANDSCAPE WITH
POPPIES
oil on canvas
h: 9; w: 12 inches
catalog no. 161

Ralph Albert Blakelock
(1847-1919)
MOONLIGHT
oil on canvas
h: 9½; w: 13½ inches
catalog no. 162

catalog no. 161

catalog no. 163

Carl Oscar Borg (1879-1947)
SPRING DAY NEAR SIMI VALLEY
oil on canvas
h: 20; w: 30½ inches
catalog no. 163

Jessie Arms Botke (1883-1971)
WHITE PEACOCK
oil on canvas
h: 30; w: 25 inches
catalog no. 164

catalog no. 164

Maurice Braun (1877-1941)
EUCALYPTUS LANDSCAPE
oil on canvas
h: 12; w: 18 inches
catalog no. 165

Maurice Braun (1877-1941)
LANDSCAPE WITH OCEAN
oil on board
h: 9; w: 12 inches
catalog no. 166

Giuseppe Leone Cadenasso
(1854-1918)
EUCALYPTUS IN A MEADOW
oil on canvas
h: 22; w: 16 inches
catalog no. 167

Giuseppe Leone Cadenasso
(1854-1918)
LANDSCAPE
oil on canvas
h: 22; w: 28 inches
catalog no. 168

William Henry Clapp
(1879-1954)
HIDDEN VALLEY ENTRANCE
oil on board
h: 7½; w: 9 inches
catalog no. 169

Alson Skinner Clark
(1876-1949)
BEACH IN SANTA MONICA,
CALIFORNIA. 1922
oil on board
h: 7; w: 9 inches
catalog no. 170

catalog no. 166

catalog no. 167

Alexis Comparet (1856-1906)
IMPRESSIONIST LANDSCAPE
oil on canvasboard
h: 11½; w: 21 inches
catalog no. 171

Gordon Coutts (1868-1937)
LANDSCAPE WITH COWS NEAR
MOUNT TAMALPAIS
oil on canvas mounted on board
h: 18; w: 24 inches
catalog no. 172

catalog no. 172

Angel DeService Espoy
(1879-1963)
Landscape with Two People
oil on board
h: 16; w: 20 inches
catalog no. 173

catalog no. 173

Charles Arthur Fries
(1854-1940)
AMONG THE WILDFLOWERS
oil on canvas
h: 16; w: 24 inches
catalog no. 174

John Marshall Gamble
(1863-1957)
POPPIES AND LUPINES (SANTA
BARBARA)
oil on canvas
h: 20¼; w: 26 inches
catalog no. 175

catalog no. 174

Selden Connor Gile
(1877-1947)
FALL TREES BY STREAM
oil on canvas
h: 11½; w: 15½ inches
catalog no. 176

Selden Connor Gile
(1877-1947)
LONE TREE
oil on canvasboard
h: 11½; w: 9½ inches
catalog no. 177

Henry Percy Gray (1869-1952)
MOON AMONG THE
EUCALYPTUS
watercolor on paper
h: 9½; w: 13 inches (sight)
catalog no. 178

Samuel Hyde Harris
(1889-1977)
MORRO BAY
oil on board
h: 8½; w: 11 inches
catalog no. 179

catalog no. 175

Samuel Hyde Harris
(1889-1977)
RENDEZVOUS
oil on board
h: 10; w: 14 inches
catalog no. 180

Anna Althea Hills (1882-1930)
EVENING GLOW, MOUNT SAN
JACINTO WITH FLOWERING
ALMOND TREES
oil on canvasboard
h: 7; w: 10 inches
catalog no. 181

Anna Althea Hills (1882-1930)
INDIAN PAINT BRUSH,
SAN JACINTO
oil on board
h: 9½; w: 13 inches
catalog no. 182

catalog no. 181

catalog no. 185

William Lees Judson
(1842-1928)
Arroyo Seco
oil on canvas
h: 16; w: 20 inches
catalog no. 183

William Lees Judson
(1842-1928)
Waning Summer. ca. 1892
oil on canvas
h: 18; w: 30 inches
catalog no. 184

Joseph Kleitsch (1885-1931)
Approaching Storm
oil on canvas
h: 12; w: 16 inches
catalog no. 185

catalog no. 184

Paul Lauritz (1889-1976)
EUCALYPTUS GROVE
oil on board
h: 22; w: 24 inches
catalog no. 186

Paul Lauritz (1889-1976)
LAVENDER HILLS, CALIFORNIA
oil on canvas
h: 15⅝; w: 19⅝ inches
catalog no. 187

Jean Mannheim (1863-1945)
AFTERNOON IN GLENDALE
oil on board
h: 12; w: 16 inches
catalog no. 188

catalog no. 186

Arthur Frank Mathews
(1860-1945)
LANDSCAPE
watercolor and gouache
h: 8½; w: 13⅓ inches
catalog no. 189

Francis John McComas
(1875-1938)
MONTEREY, CALIFORNIA. 1901
watercolor on paper
h: 14½; w: 19 inches
catalog no. 190

Thomas Arnold McGlynn
(1878-1966)
CALIFORNIA OAK TREE
oil on canvas
h: 25; w: 27 inches
catalog no. 191

Thomas Arnold McGlynn
(1878-1966)
ROLLING HILLS WITH HOUSES
oil on canvas laid down on
board
h: 25¼; w: 27¼ inches
catalog no. 192

catalog no. 192

Edgar Alwin Payne (1883-1947)
CALIFORNIA LANDSCAPE
oil on board
h: 11; w: 15 inches
catalog no. 193

Edgar Alwin Payne (1883-1947)
HIGH SIERRAS LAKE AND
MOUNTAINS
oil on board
h: 11½; w: 14 inches
catalog no. 194

Edgar Alwin Payne (1883-1947)
LAGUNA CANYON
oil on canvas
h: 15½; w: 20 inches
catalog no. 195

catalog no. 195

Gottardo Fidele Ponziano
Piazzoni (1872-1945)
LAKE TAHOE. 1912
oil on board
h: 8; w: 5¾ inches
catalog no. 196

William Merritt Post
(1856-1935)
LANDSCAPE WITH TREES AND
STREAM
oil on canvas
h: 18; w: 24 inches
catalog no. 197

Hanson Duvall Puthuff
(1875-1972)
GROVE IN AUTUMN
oil on board
h: 10; w: 12 inches
catalog no. 198

catalog no. 198

Granville Richard Seymour
Redmond (1871-1935)
EARLY MOONRISE
oil on canvas
h: 8; w: 10 inches
catalog no. 199

Granville Richard Seymour
Redmond (1871-1935)
NOCTURNAL MOON
oil on board
h: 8¾; w: 12⅜ inches
catalog no. 200

catalog no. 201

Christian Siemer (1874-1940)
JOSHUA TREE, SAN GORGONIO
oil on canvas
h: 25; w: 36 inches
catalog no. 201

William Posey Silva
(1859-1948)
CARMEL MISSION. 1941
oil on canvas
h: 25; w: 30 inches
catalog no. 202

Frederick Carl Smith
(1868-1955)
WHERE SAND MEETS EARTH
(LAGUNA BEACH)
oil on board
h: 10¾; w: 13⅕ inches
catalog no. 203

Charles Volkmar (1841-1914)
LANDSCAPE. 1878
oil on canvas laid down on
board
h: 9¾; w: 14 inches
catalog no. 204

catalog no. 202

Elmer Wachtel (1864-1929)
LANDSCAPE
oil on canvas
h: 14; w: 18 inches
catalog no. 205

Elmer Wachtel (1864-1929)
VALLEY VISTA
oil on canvas
h: 12; w: 16 inches
catalog no. 206

Elmer Wachtel (1864-1929)
WILD LUPINE
oil on canvas
h: 13; w: 17 inches
catalog no. 207

Marion Kavanaugh Wachtel
(1876-1954)
THE ARROYO, LATE AFTERNOON
oil on canvasboard
h: 12; w: 10 inches
catalog no. 208

Marion Kavanaugh Wachtel
(1876-1954)
ARROYO SECO
oil on canvasboard
h: 16; w: 20 inches
catalog no. 209

catalog no. 208

Marion Kavanaugh Wachtel
(1876-1954)
SANTA ANITA
oil on canvasboard
h: 12⅝; w: 20 inches
catalog no. 210

Marion Kavanaugh Wachtel
(1876-1954)
SELF PORTRAIT
oil on board
h: 15; w: 10 inches
catalog no. 211

William Wendt (1865-1946)
CALIFORNIA HILLS
oil on canvas
h: 25; w: 30 inches
catalog no. 212

catalog no. 212

William Wendt (1865-1946)
MEMORY LANE. 1919
oil on canvas
h: 24; w: 36 inches
catalog no. 213

Theodore Wores (1859-1939)
CALIFORNIA LANDSCAPE WITH
FLOWERING TREES
oil on board
h: 9¼; w: 12½ inches
catalog no. 214

catalog no. 214

Native American Art

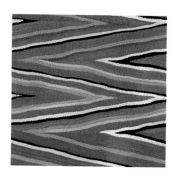

Many Native Americans speak of art as a way of approaching the world rather than as beautiful objects designed for their own sake. "Objects like people, project beauty or harmony outward, but they are dynamic rather than static, and they are primarily important not in themselves but as manifestations of harmonious, good living."[6]

Collections of Native American art seem to evoke particularly strong feelings. The Sheldon collection of Native American objects is guided by a unique attitude and philosophy.

At the turn of the twentieth century, the general perception that Indian ways were of the past generated popular enthusiasm to collect even a small memento of a vanishing lifestyle. Collectors sought Indian basketry, weaving, pottery and other objects, and Native Americans across the country responded. Not only did traditional artforms continue to thrive, but in some cases dormant traditions were actually revived, the Hopi pottery in Arizona, for example.

Indian items were seen in turn-of-the-century interiors. Articles and advertisements suggesting decorative uses for Indian baskets appeared in *House Beautiful* and other related periodicals in 1898, 1902 and 1909.[7]

Much of the stimulation for this decoration came from the design philosophy of the American Arts and Crafts Movement, whose proponents believed that a well-designed environment could promote harmony and well-being. They favored hand-crafted items of natural materials rather than machine-made products. The aesthetic also preferred simple, unadorned surfaces and geometric forms.

Gustav Stickley assured readers in his monthly magazine *The Craftsman* that Indian objects, especially geometrically patterned rugs and baskets, were worthy of ownership. Furniture in his New York showrooms was also adorned with artifacts.

By around 1915 the Indian object-collecting craze and interest in the American Arts and Crafts interiors were diminishing as a new and quieter discussion of Native American art emerged in segments of the art community. By the late 1920s the beginning of yet another revival of Indian art emerged in the Southwest, especially in Santa Fe and Taos, New Mexico.

The Sheldons are particularly attracted to older Navajo and Pueblo wearing blankets. The nineteenth-century Navajo-made blankets for functional use as outer garments were so admired by other tribes that they became popular trade items. With the arrival of the Americans in Navajo territory, the social and political upheaval was reflected in rapid changes in the style and materials of the blankets. Significantly, the Sheldon collection is carefully composed of fine examples of the Navajo Stripe, Chief and Serape wearing blankets, along with occasional examples of Pueblo and Spanish weaving.

The basic design format of a Navajo blanket is traditionally a stripe or band, an outgrowth of the ancient Pueblo weaving tradition. Three phases mark the development of the Chief Blanket: The First Phase design consists only of stripes, the Second Phase has rectangular block designs inserted within the stripes to create a grid, and the Third Phase has blocks that evolve into diamond motifs.

During the late 1860s, there was a shift in the approach to the Serape, a style of blanket based on Spanish/Mexican precedents. The Serape is the only classic Navajo blanket that was not an adaptation of a Pueblo model. Spanish colonists in New Mexico wore a garment called the Saltillo Serape, so-named after the village in northern Mexico where it originated. The Navajo greatly simplified the Spanish/Mexican model by enlarging the elements.

The Serape design elements evolved into the Eye-Dazzler, the last stage in the development of the blanket. Eye-Dazzler is a general term for blankets of bright colors and optical patterns, woven with handspun native wool synthetically dyed by the weaver, or with commercially dyed Germantown yarns.

[6]Gary Witherspoon, *Language and Art in the Navajo Universe* (Ann Arbor: University of Michigan Press, 1977), p. 23, pp. 151-152.

[7]George Wharton James, "Indian Baskets in House Decoration," *The Chautauquan* 33 (1901): 619; Charles Otto Thieme, "Collecting Navajo Weaving," in Otto Thieme, Ruth E. Franzen and Sally G. Kabat, eds., *Collecting Navajo Weaving* (Minneapolis: Goldstein Gallery, University of Minnesota, 1984), pp. 2-3.

Among the Pueblo pottery represented in the collection are Acoma, Zuni and San Ildefonso pieces. Part of the late nineteenth-century Pueblo pottery revival was based on motifs and forms found on remains of prehistoric pots from the various Pueblos.

Notable baskets in the collection include rare examples by some of California's greatest basketmakers — the Cahuilla, Chemehuevi, Pomo and Washo.

Native American art is bound with cultural associations and assumptions. It is the power of the Indian vision and spirit that is translated in the pieces, which then engenders interest and creates an emotional response for avid collectors. *K.P.H.*

catalog no. 237 (left basket), catalog no. 216 (right basket), catalog no. 230 (blanket)

Acoma Pueblo
POLYCHROME OLLA. ca. 1900
ceramic
h: 10; dia: 12 inches
catalog no. 215

Apache
COILED BASKET OLLA
willow and devil's claw
h: 10; dia: 12 inches
catalog no. 216

Apache
WAR SHIRT
beaded and fringed hide with
pigment and human hair
l: 40; w: 64 inches
catalog no. 217

Cahuilla
COILED SNAKE BASKET TRAY
sumac and juncus
h: 1; dia: 15½ inches
catalog no. 218

Cahuilla
COILED SNAKE BASKET BOWL
sumac, natural and dyed juncus
h: 3¼; w: 8½; l: 9¾ inches
catalog no. 219

Chemehuevi
COILED BASKET OLLA. ca. 1910
willow and devil's claw
h: 7; dia: 8 inches
catalog no. 220

Mexican
SALTILLO SERAPE. ca. 1900
wool; red, black, ivory, yellow,
indigo blue
l: 94; w: 47 inches
catalog no. 221

catalog no. 215

catalog no. 232 (blanket), catalog no. 220 (left basket), catalog no. 218 (right basket), catalog no. 219 (far right basket)

Mexican
SALTILLO SERAPE
wool; indigo blue, brown, ivory,
pale green
l: 91; w: 54 inches
catalog no. 222

catalog no. 222

Navajo
BAYETA SERAPE. ca. 1870s
wool; dark red, pale red, sage
green, black, ivory
l: 73; w: 49 inches
catalog no. 223

Navajo
BLUE TWILL MANTA. 1875
wool; indigo blue, bayeta red,
green
l: 54; w: 37 inches
catalog no. 224

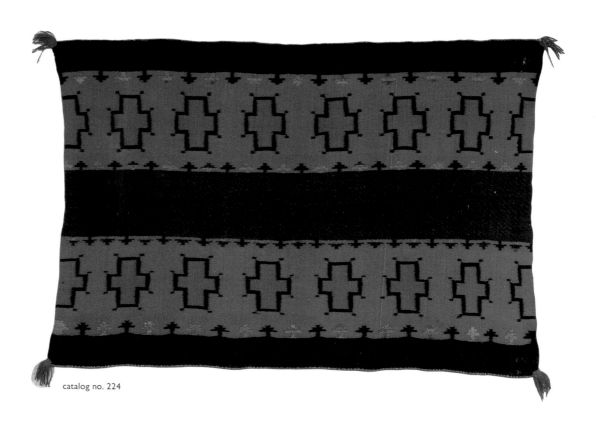

catalog no. 224

Navajo
CLASSIC BABY'S WEARING
BLANKET. ca. 1860s
wool; indigo blue, red, ivory,
sage green, pale orange
l: 31; w: 24 inches
catalog no. 225

Navajo
CLOTH STRIP MOKI. 1865
wool; indigo blue, bayeta red,
white, brown, green
l: 51; w: 76 inches
catalog no. 226

Navajo
GERMANTOWN SAMPLER
wool; red, indigo blue, green,
gold, yellow, maroon, purple
l: 17½; w: 17½ inches
catalog no. 227

Navajo
GERMANTOWN SAMPLER
wool; red, indigo blue, green,
white, maroon, gold
l: 17½; w: 17½ inches
catalog no. 228

Navajo
GERMANTOWN EYE-DAZZLER
BLANKET
wool; red, sage green, ivory,
black, purple
l: 53; w: 39 inches
catalog no. 229

catalog no. 225

catalog no. 226

Navajo
LATE CLASSIC CHILD'S
WEARING BLANKET. ca. 1875
wool; indigo blue, red, ivory
l: 53; w: 34 inches
catalog no. 230

Navajo
LATE CLASSIC GERMANTOWN
WEARING BLANKET.
ca. 1870-1880
wool; black, red, ivory, indigo
blue
l: 84; w: 52 inches
catalog no. 231

Navajo
LATE CLASSIC WOMAN'S
WEARING BLANKET. 1875
wool; red, indigo blue, yellow,
black, ivory, green
l: 61½; w: 43 inches
catalog no. 232

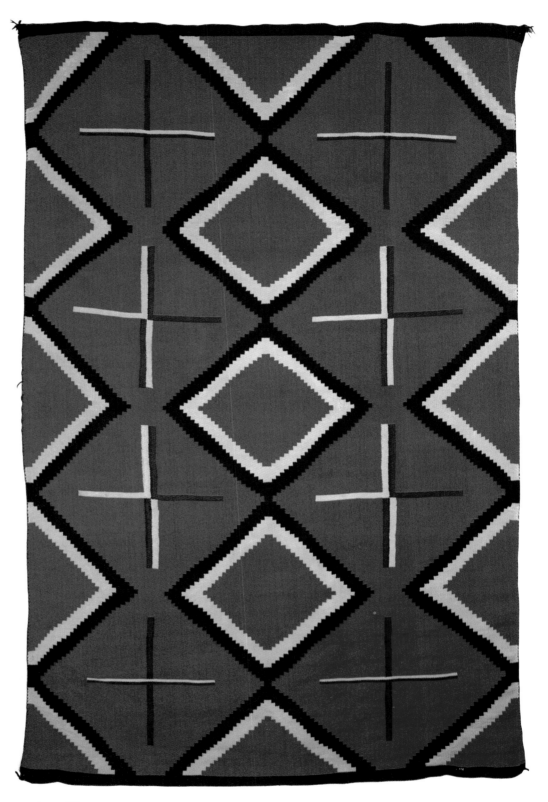

catalog no. 231

Navajo
THIRD PHASE CHIEF'S BLANKET.
ca. 1890
wool; red, ivory, dark brown,
dark grey
l: 70; w: 52 inches
catalog no. 233

Navajo
WEDGEWEAVE BLANKET.
ca. 1860s
wool; red, orange, ivory, black,
pale brown
l: 87; w: 56 inches
catalog no. 234

New Mexican
RIO GRANDE STRIPED BLANKET.
1880-1890
wool; indigo blue, ivory, brown
l: 89; w: 44½ inches
catalog no. 235

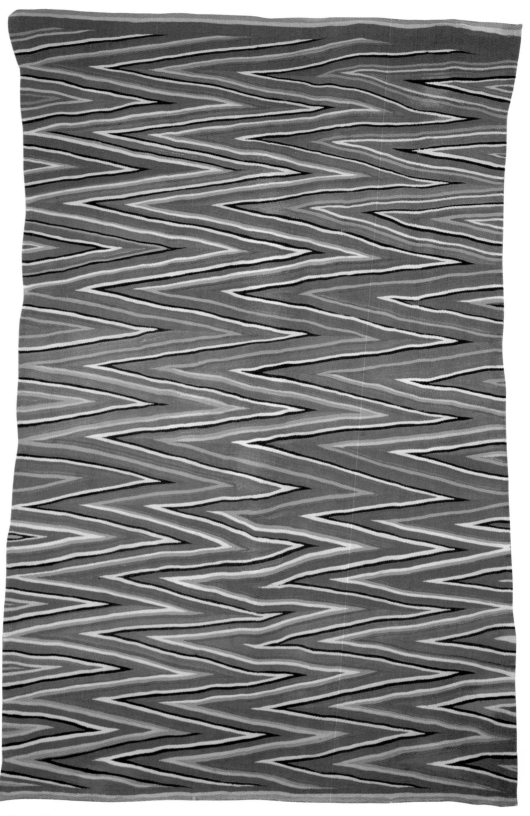

catalog no. 234

catalog no. 238

catalog no. 240

Pomo
COILED FEATHER BASKET
willow, sedge grass root, quail
top knots, mallard duck and
meadowlark feathers and clam
shell beads
h: 2½; dia: 5¾ inches
catalog no. 236

Pomo
COILED GIFT BASKET
willow, sedge grass root and
dyed bullrush
h: 2½; w: 4¼; l: 5¼ inches
catalog no. 237

San Ildefonso Pueblo
Maria Martinez (1884-1980)
LIDDED BOX
ceramic, matte and polished
blackware
h: 4; w: 5; d: 3½ inches
catalog no. 238

Washo
Tootsie Dick Sam
COILED BASKET BOWL.
ca. 1913-1918
peeled willow, redbud and dyed
bracken fern root
h: 10; dia. 21 inches
catalog no. 239

Washo
COILED BIRD BASKET BOWL
peeled willow, redbud and dyed
bracken fern root
h: 5; dia: 9½ inches
catalog no. 240

catalog no. 239

Zuni Pueblo
POLYCHROME OLLA
ceramic
h: 9½; dia: 12 inches
catalog no. 241

Zuni Pueblo
MOKI STRIPED BLANKET.
ca. 1870-1885
wool; indigo blue, ivory, brown
l: 67; w: 47 inches
catalog no. 242

Zuni Pueblo
MOKI BLANKET. ca. 1865-1875
wool; indigo blue, brown, bayeta
red, white, green
l: 73; w: 57 inches
catalog no. 243

catalog no. 241 (olla), catalog no. 242 (blanket)

catalog no. 243

Selected Bibliography

Adams, Steven. *The Arts and Crafts Movement.* Secaucus, NJ: Quintet Publishing, Ltd., 1987.

Andersen, Timothy J., Eudorah M. Moore and Robert W. Winter, eds. *California Design 1910.* Salt Lake City: Peregrine Smith Books, 1989.

Berlant, Anthony and Mary Hunt Kahlenberg. *Walk in Beauty: The Navajo and Their Blankets.* Salt Lake City: Peregrine Smith Books, 1977.

Bowman, Leslie Greene. *American Arts and Crafts: Virtue in Design.* Los Angeles: Los Angeles County Museum of Art, 1990.

Bray, Hazel W. *The Potter's Art in California 1885 to 1955.* Oakland: The Oakland Museum Art Department, 1980.

Chelette, Iona M., Katherine Plake Hough and Will South. *California Grandeur and Genre: From the Collection of James L. Coran and Walter A. Nelson-Rees.* Palm Springs, CA: Palm Springs Desert Museum, 1991.

Cincinnati Art Galleries. *The Glover Collection: The David W. and Katherine M. Glover Collection of Rookwood Pottery.* Cincinnati: Cincinnati Art Galleries, 1991.

Clark, Garth. *American Ceramics: 1876 to the Present.* New York: Abbeville Press, 1987.

Cooper-Hewitt Museum. *American Art Pottery.* Washington, DC: The Smithsonian Institution, 1987.

Cumming, Elizabeth and Wendy Kaplan. *The Arts and Crafts Movement.* London and New York: Thames and Hudson, Ltd., 1991.

Cummins, Virginia Raymond. *Rookwood Pottery Potpourri.* Cincinnati: Cincinnati Art Galleries, 1991.

Darling, Sharon S. *Teco: Art Pottery of the Prairie School.* Erie, PA: Erie Art Museum, 1989.

Dietz, Ulysses G. *The Newark Museum Collection of American Art Pottery.* Newark, NJ: The Newark Museum, 1984.

Eidelberg, Martin. *From Our Native Clay.* New York: Turn of the Century Editions, 1987.

Fidler, Patricia J. *Art with a Mission: Objects of the Arts and Crafts Movement.* Lawrence: Spencer Museum of Art, The University of Kansas, 1991.

Gray, Stephen, ed. *A Catalog of the Roycrofters.* New York: Turn of the Century Editions, 1989.

Gray, Stephen. *The Early Work of Gustav Stickley.* New York: Turn of the Century Editions, 1987.

Gray, Stephen, ed. *Gustav Stickley after 1909.* New York: Turn of the Century Editions, 1990.

Gray, Stephen, ed. *The Mission Furniture of L. & J. G. Stickley.* Revised Edition. New York: Turn of the Century Editions, 1989.

Gray, Stephen and Robert Edwards, eds. *Collected Works of Gustav Stickley.* New York: Turn of the Century Editions, 1981.

Henzke, Lucile. *Art Pottery of America.* Exton, PA: Schiffer Publishing, Ltd., 1982.

James, George Wharton. *Indian Basketry.* 4th ed. New York: Dover Publications, Inc., 1972.

James, George Wharton. *Indian Blankets & Their Makers.* New York: Dover Publications, Inc., 1974.

Jones, Harvey L. *Mathews, Masterpieces of the California Decorative Style*. Oakland: Gibbs M. Smith, Inc. in association with The Oakland Museum, 1985.

Kaplan, Wendy. *"The Art that is Life": The Arts and Crafts Movement in America, 1875-1920*. Boston: Museum of Fine Arts, 1987.

Keen, Kirsten Hoving. *American Art Pottery 1875-1930*. Wilmington, DE: Delaware Art Museum, 1978.

Koch, Robert. *Louis C. Tiffany's Glass Bronzes Lamps*. New York: Crown Publishers, 1971.

Linoff, Victor M., ed. *Illustrated Mission Furniture Catalog, 1912-1913*. New York: Dover Publications, Inc., 1991.

Ludwig, Coy L. *The Arts & Crafts Movement in New York State 1890s-1920s*. Hamilton, NY: Gallery Association of New York State, Inc., 1983.

Makinson, Randell, L. *Greene & Greene: Architecture as a Fine Art*. Salt Lake City: Peregrine Smith, Inc., 1977.

Makinson, Randell, L. *Greene & Greene: Furniture and Related Designs*. Salt Lake City: Peregrine Smith, Inc., 1979.

Marek, Don. *Arts and Crafts Furniture Design*. Grand Rapids, MI: Grand Rapids Art Museum, 1987.

Marek, Don. *Charles P. Limbert Company*. New York: Turn of the Century Editions, 1981.

McConnell, Kevin. *Heintz Art Metal: Silver-on-Bronze Wares*. West Chester, PA: Schiffer Publishing, Ltd., 1990.

McDonald, Ann Gilbert. *All About Weller*. Marietta, OH: Antique Publications, 1989.

Naylor, Gillian, et al. *The Encyclopedia of Arts and Crafts: The International Art Movement, 1850-1920*. New York: E.P. Dutton, 1989.

New Orleans Museum of Art. *Creative Clays: American Art Pottery from the New Orleans Museum of Art*. New Orleans: New Orleans Museum of Art, 1992.

Peck, Herbert. *The Book of Rookwood Pottery*. New York: Crown Publishers, 1968; Cincinnati: Cincinnati Art Galleries, 1991.

Peck, Herbert. *The Second Book of Rookwood Pottery*. Tucson: Herbert Peck, 1985.

Perry, Barbara, ed. *American Ceramics*. New York: Rizzoli International Publications, Inc., 1989.

Poesch, Jessie. *Newcomb Pottery: An Enterprise for Southern Women, 1895-1940*. Exton, PA: Schiffer Publishing, Ltd., 1984.

Rasnick, Richard M. and Eugene Hecht. *Teco: Hints for Gifts and Home Decoration*. Terra Cotta, IL: The Gates Potteries, 1905; Madison: Razmataz Press.

Sonoma County Museum. *So Here Cometh: California and the Arts & Crafts Ideal*. Santa Rosa, CA: Sonoma County Museum, 1991.

Stickley, Gustav. *The 1912 and 1915 Gustav Stickley Craftsman Furniture Catalogs*. A Joint Publication of The Athanaeum of Philadelphia and Dover Publications, Inc., New York, 1991.

Trapp, Kenneth R. *Ode to Nature: Flowers and Landscapes of the Rookwood Pottery 1880-1940*. New York: The Jordan-Volpe Gallery, 1980.

Unabridged Reprints of Two Mission Furniture Catalogs: Craftsman Furniture Made by Gustav Stickley and The Work of L. & J. G. Stickley. New York: Dover Publications, Inc., 1979.

Volpe, Tod M. and Beth Cathers. *Treasures of the American Arts and Crafts Movement, 1890-1920*. New York: Harry N. Abrams, 1988.

Wilson, Richard Guy. *From Architecture to Object: Masterworks of the American Arts & Crafts Movement*. New York: Dutton Studio Books, 1991.

Palm Springs Desert Museum

Photography
Grey Crawford, South Pasadena, California

Catalog Design
Lilli Colton Design, Glendale, California

Text set in Weiss and Gill Sans by
Central Typesetting Company,
Los Angeles
Display type set in Willow by
Aldus Type Studios,
Los Angeles

Printed on Quintessence by Typecraft, Inc.,
Pasadena, California